Where The Fire Went

**A Collection of Poems, Parables, &
Perspectives**

Where The Fire Went

A Collection of Poems, Parables, & Perspectives

by
Amira Jennah

For my children, who are the light I rise for and the love that grounds me. May you always know your voice holds power. For my friends, who held me when I couldn't hold myself. Your presence has been a balm, your laughter, a lifeline. Finally, for those who inspired these pages. Some who stayed, some who left, and some who never knew the depth of their imprint. You lit the match. These words are the fire that followed.

With all my love

Amira Jennah

Table of Contents

Acknowledgement

To write this book was to walk through fire and come out ash-covered, but whole. I could not have done it alone.

To my children, thank you for being my greatest reason to rise. Your laughter, love, and light continue to remind me what truly matters.

To my friends, the ones who answered late-night calls, sat with me in silence, and reminded me of my worth when I forgot. Thank you for seeing me, hearing me, and holding me.

To those who inspired these pages,

whether by love or heartbreak, thank you. Your presence and your absence gave me something to write about. Some of you were poems. Some were parables. All of you were necessary.

To every reader who finds a piece of themselves in these words, may they bring you comfort, clarity, and courage. May they remind you that the fire inside you may flicker, but it never truly dies.

Finally, to the version of me that kept going, I see you. I honor you. I love you.

Preface

Where the Fire Went is more than a collection of poetry and reflections, it's a record of survival, rebirth, and remembering who I am.

These pages were born from tired mornings and sleepless nights, from heartbreak that almost swallowed me and the hope that lit me back up. They came from the messy middle, from the in-between space of letting go, and learning how to hold myself again.

I did not write this book with the intention of being brave. I wrote it because I had no choice. The pain had to go somewhere. The silence was too overwhelming. Writing became the only way I knew how to pray.

The poems, parables, and perspectives in this book are in no particular order, just like healing. They are as random, chaotic, and beautiful as I am. Some were written in moments of clarity, others in the midst of confusion. All of them are honest. All of them are mine.

In these words, you'll find love that left, grief that lingered, and joy that still insisted on returning. You'll witness the soft power of healing. The kind that walks with the past and still dares to bloom.

If you've ever wondered where your own fire went, I hope you find flickers of it here and that it leads you back to yourself.

~ Amira Jennah

Don't Be Her

Don't be her
The girl who gets taken advantage of
Taken for granted
Work all day
Then straight home to cook & clean
Be everything he say he never had and
need
All while he's cheating
You in the house, don't run the streets
Yet his mind and/or body is still in
someone else's sheets
He knows he's wrong
So he place all negativity on you
Apparently, you're crazy
Seeing things you didn't see
Hearing things you didn't hear
And
Doctored receipts
It's giving

Unwarranted insecurities
And attempts at making you second guess
yourself
No, don't be her
Is he even worth it?
Your sanity
Consistently trying to convince yourself
he'll change
He'll be a better man one day
Once he realizes what he has in you
Everything will be ok
I don't know, maybe you are insane
Trying to hold on to something that left
you a long time ago
Forgetting who the hell you are
Allowing anyone to place you in their
pocket
And fiddle you when they feel like it
I said don't be her
Nah sis
Don't let him call you sacred while keeping
you a secret
Why he got you tucked away?

Talking about he want you all to himself
You ain't no show pony
No prize to present
No post for likes
Or simply a warm body
To come home to at night
Don't be her
You better pick your head up
Stop letting him put you down
Start smiling all the time
Don't let him see you frown
Matter fact
Put him on the block list sis
When he asks why he can't get through to
you
Say, "Same reason I can't get through to
you!"
Better give some cold shoulders
Put an icebox where your heart used to be
No beats
Let him know
It's cold out there in them streets
But you Arctic now

Let him fall with the rubble, man
Save yourself the trouble man
Don't feel bad you chose yourself
You owe yourself!
Pack your shit
Build your own castles
Grant your own wishes
And when he's down on his knees
Begging and pleading
With the look of defeat
Trying to figure out why you're leaving
Chuck the deuces
Control, alt, delete

The Girl & The River

There once was a girl who stood by a river, clutching a glass bottle with a message sealed inside. "This is my hope," she whispered. "If I hold it tightly enough, the current won't take it. Maybe the one I wrote it for will come back. Maybe they'll read it and understand."

She waited for days. Then weeks. Seasons passed. Her feet grew roots in the riverbank, and still she held the bottle, her hands trembling from exhaustion. One morning, an old woman passed by and asked, "Child, why do you look so tired?" The girl answered, "I'm keeping this hope alive. If I let go, it will drift away, and I'll have nothing." The old woman smiled gently. "Hope tied to what we can't change is just grief in pretty clothing."

The girl looked at how tightly she'd been holding the bottle. She saw the imprint it left in her skin. The way the glass kept her from touching the water, from feeling the life moving all around her. With a deep breath, she opened her fingers. The bottle floated out onto the river, carried gently by the current, not lost, just released. For the first time, she stepped into the river. Not to chase anything. Not even to hold on.

But simply to move.

Sometimes grief wears the mask of hope...

We hold on to what might be and not what is. The apology that never came, the person they could become, the life we imagined unfolding differently. But hope, when it's tethered to denial, quietly

7

becomes grief in disguise. An ache for a future we can't control. There comes a moment that's not dramatic or loud. Where you finally stop reaching. The moment when clarity finally hits you. You surrender to the truth. The truth that the future is not yours to bend. That healing isn't about holding on, it's about letting go. What happens when you do? The energy shifts.

You exhale.

You rise.

Don't carry hope like a burden, move forward in freedom.

This isn't giving up.

It's growing up.

Sunshine

He brings her sunshine when her rain
clouds are overflowing
He knew she needed just a little bit of rain
to wash away the tears and the pain
But when the rain wouldn't stop, he told
the sun to take reign
The clouds parted ways for the warm rays
to cover her spirits and lift her out of her
dismay
Her heart beats for him
Her soul speaks to him
So, he makes sure she keeps a smile
Because her smile lights his life, and his life
lights her smile
They keep a balance for the universe
He needs her as she needs him
When they are together, there is still no
them Bonded forever like a rose to its stem
She blooms via him
And when the day turns to dusk, and the
world starts to dim

He sends the moon up to the heavens just
to brighten her again
He sings to her through the birds, and the
wind carries the words
Making sure they reach her quickly
He soothes her with his melody and she
sways to his beat
She dances on his heart
He loves the pitter patter of her feet
No room for insecurity
Their love is one of a kind
A divine, refined frame of mind
Like nonalcoholic wine
They know their mind could never be
inclined to go any other way than their
matrimony vine
So they only indulge in the berries of their
own bush
And it produces through every season
But true love is the strongest reason that
neither of them will ever be leaving each
other's side

A love like this could only be through the
power of the Most High
A love like this, I wish was mine
A love like this probably doesn't even exist
But I'd like to keep an open mind

Let no corrupt communication proceed out of your mouth, but that which is good to the use of edifying, that it may minister grace unto the hearers.

~Ephesians 4:29

Sacrifice

How much of yourself are you willing to
sacrifice?
Is the cost of acceptance your mere
existence?
If they tell you that you can't breathe
Will you suffocate and die?
Will you cry yourself to sleep every night
At the wonder of what free will feels like?
How you let them take your birthright?
You crawled into this world with nothing
except your body
How easily we let them take ownership of
our bodies
Imagine the looks on your ancestors' faces
Who rose up against their masters
Only for you to bow down now
Call yourself royalty?
Who gave you that crown?

Who told you the worth layered the cloth
on your body?
Who told you your speech was only
acceptable if it's "proper?"
Who placed you on that pedestal and then
knocked you over?
Who gave you that frown?
And that chip on your shoulder?
Who told you that you were no good?
Who called you beautiful and then put a
mask on you anyway?
Who told you your life was only worth the
wages they paid?
Who mined through your thighs in search
of their gold
And still took the pot at the end of the
rainbow?
Who pushed your buttons and then
labeled you crazy?
Held you down and then called you lazy?
Wrapped you up
Straight jacket
Gave you pills

Then called you an addict?
Who told you to accept
And then endear
The names that they gave you?
Tell you, you ain't God
Still in secret, they praise you?
Isn't it odd?
How they practice sovereignty
But are the loudest in the room
When there's talk of inequality?
All the world's a stage
Men and women merely players
Race and Ethnicity
Those are the layers
See they hate us for our righteousness
Most want to be us
So, they copy and paste
We call it appropriate
Openly they hate
Yet, our culture they take
Ivory Wash our history
Our history misplaced
We feel defeated

Yet they've won no case
Isn't it odd?
How they practice sovereignty
But aren't the loudest in the room
When there's talk of inequality?

The Mirror in the Dust

There once was a village nestled in a valley where the people had long forgotten their origin. Generations ago, their ancestors were kings and queens, builders of temples, keepers of stars, and speakers of divine truth. But over time, invaders came with stories instead of swords.

These new stories whispered into the villagers' ears, telling them they were born broken, that their skin was stained, their language uncivil, their joy too loud, their pain too much. The villagers were told to change their names, straighten their backs, close their mouths, and wear masks shaped like someone else's idea of perfection.

So, they did. They forgot their fire. They bowed their heads in the name of peace.

But one day, a child curious and untrained in the art of forgetting wandered into the forest beyond the valley. There, beneath layers of dust and vines, the child found an ancient mirror carved from obsidian and gold. When she looked into it, she didn't see herself as she had always known, tired, small, apologetic. No. She saw her ancestors standing behind her, fierce and proud, with eyes like galaxies and heartbeats of thunder.

The mirror whispered to the child, "Remember…" At that moment, the child remembered everything. The language. The power. The name.

She returned to the village, held the mirror high, and said:
"You are not what they say you are."

Some turned away, afraid of the truth.

But many others came forward.
They saw.
They wept.
They rose.

And from that day forward, no one walked
with their head bowed again.

Freedom

It's not just walking away from what no longer serves you. It's reclaiming your power after life tried to break you. I've loved deeply, lost painfully, and risen quietly, even with tears in my eyes. I've been misunderstood, mistreated, and overlooked... But I've never let that stop me from choosing joy. Freedom is waking up with a heavy heart and still choosing to smile.

It's holding space for grief and hope at the same time. It's trusting God and the Universe even when the path is dark and unclear. I've fought for peace within myself. I've learned how to let go, how to surrender, how to keep going. Life didn't get easier, but I got stronger.

This is the freedom I live in now. No matter what tried to break you. You're still worthy of light, of love, of joy. Smile anyway. Believe anyway. Rise anyway, because your freedom is not just survival, *it's your rebirth*.

Waiting

I didn't fall in love with you
I walked into it
Step by hesitant step
Like barefoot through broken glass
Aware of every shard
But still…
Still choosing to bleed a little
You never promised forever
You barely promised tomorrow
Your eyes spoke in echoes
And your hands held the world like it was
too heavy to carry
Like it might drop if you grip it too tight
And I…
I offered my heart anyway
You
With your bright smile
And your soul locked behind bolted doors
You

With trauma etched into your silence
And healing that doesn't come on anyone's
Timeline but your own
You told me you weren't ready
Not for this
Not for me
And still…
You let me stay
Just for a moment as your beloved
That transitioned into something softer
A friend
A maybe
A "someday" wrapped in uncertainty
I see you, love
I see the war behind your eyes
I see the boy who learned to flinch before
he spoke
Who learned that loving too much
Meant losing yourself
And I don't want to be another battlefield
So I wait
Not like some passive prayer
Waiting for you to notice me

But like a rooted tree
Patient with the seasons
Grateful for the sun when it shows
Content to weather the cold when it
doesn't
Because you've already given me so much
The way you listen
Really listen
Like I'm poetry in motion
The way we laugh at midnight
About nothing at all
The way your presence calms the chaos
Even when your own world is spinning
I will not rush your becoming
I will not demand love from a heart still
learning how to hold itself
But I will be here
Quietly
Steadily
Loving you without needing you to match
it
Not now
Not yet

Maybe not ever
And if someday comes
If you find the strength to hand me your
heart whole and unguarded
Know that mine never left
It just waited
Wrapped in hope
Braided with patience
Softened by gratitude
Until then
I'll love you in the ways you can accept
As a friend
As peace when the world turns cruel
And maybe that's enough
Maybe it has to be
But still
still…
I'm here

Sometimes waiting for someone can feel like a burden...

It can feel like you're not a priority. Like their indecision is selfish. In some cases, maybe it is. However, sometimes, it's also self-awareness. It takes maturity to admit when you're not ready for love, even if that truth disappoints someone who cares.

Still, if waiting begins to hurt more than it helps, it might be time to let go. You don't have to stop loving them. You just have to start choosing you.

Self-preservation is not selfish. It's the first law of nature. Your well-being matters more than any imagined future with someone who isn't ready now. We can't control timing, and we can't control other people's choices. What we can do is surrender to what is, and that surrender often brings the peace we've been searching for.

Letting go isn't a loss. Sometimes, it's the beginning of clarity.

Love is patient and kind; love does not envy or boast; it is not arrogant or rude. It does not insist on its own way; it is not irritable or resentful; it does not rejoice at wrongdoing but rejoices with the truth. Love bears all things, believes all things, hopes all things, endures all things. Love never ends. As for prophecies, they will pass away; as for tongues, they will cease; as for knowledge, it will pass away.

~ 1 Corinthians 13:4-8

God Don't Like Ugly

God don't like ugly
Ain't talking about the opposite of pretty
either
But when your negativity cuts through the
air, it's lethal
You carry around loaded clips
Then, like to release them on other people
What reward do you get for bringing
others down?
You spread frowns like a plague
When you walk into the room, everyone
else scatters away
Don't you think it's time for a change?
How beautiful you would be if you spread
joy instead of pain
If you just took a look inside
Instead of trying to shift the blame

Imagine the display of smiles you'd bring
I mean, ain't you tired?
Ain't you tired of walking around with all
that bad energy
The world is beautiful
So, you should be inspired
Connecting with your community
Synergy
Have you ever heard of karma?
Don't you know that you reap what you
sow
They say beauty is in the eye of the
beholder
Your face distorts at every toxic blow
The face once called fine now looks
horrible
Disdain fills the hearts of everyone that
comes around you
Shooting your anger all over the place
Now everybody catching strays
Caught up your case
Living with your forever blues
But listen closely

I'm trying to help you
Every day begins the promise of new
beginning
So, stop dimming your own light
And maybe your world will start spinning
right
There is an art to living with joy, you just
have to paint a positive picture
Start giving compliments instead of
complaints
And watch your life get richer
Start reading some scripture
Take the good, leave the bad
Discernment is the elixir
Life is way too short to be walking around
mean-mugging
Plus God don't like ugly
We ain't talking about the opposite of
pretty either
I'm talking about mean and aunry like
what we used to call an old geezer
So let go of that hurt and be truly you
Be Beautiful

The Energy You Carry

There was a woman named Kayla who walked through life like a walking thunderstorm. She wasn't ugly, not in the way people usually think, but her energy was. Heavy. Loud. Unchecked. Every room she entered shifted. Laughter died down. People kept conversations short. Group chats went silent when she joined. Kayla thought the world just couldn't handle her "realness." The truth was simple: she was bitter. She was hurt, not honest.

She confused being intimidating with being powerful. Every post was a complaint. Every compliment was backhanded. Every story she told ended with how someone "did her dirty."

Then one day, she went viral, except not in a good way. Someone recorded her lashing out at a cashier who made a small mistake. The video was everywhere. Comments flooded in:

"This is the type of energy that ruins your whole day."

"No wonder nobody wants to be around her."

"Sis needs therapy, not an attitude."

It hit her harder than she expected. At first, she defended herself. "They don't know me!" she posted. Even her own circle fell quiet. Some unfollowed. A few messaged her with love, but it didn't feel like enough. Then, she saw a comment that made her self-evaluate:

"Hurt people hurt people. But healed people heal people. Which one do you wanna be?"

That night, Kayla couldn't sleep. She replayed her past few months... arguments, cold stares, being alone in crowds. She realized that she had become someone she didn't even like being around. So, she did something small the next day. She smiled at the coffee shop barista. She said "thank you" to the bus driver. She messaged a friend just to say she appreciated them.

It felt weird at first, like wearing shoes that didn't fit, but slowly the energy shifted. Weeks passed, and people started noticing. She posted a photo with the caption:
"Trying joy on for size. Might keep it."

The barista knew her name now and asked about her day. Her group chats lit back up. She even got invited out more. She changed for herself. She changed for others. She finally let go of what was poisoning her spirit. Although life wasn't perfect, Kayla was lighter. Softer. Still her, but better.

Because at the end of the day?
God don't like ugly.
It was never about looks.
It was about the energy you carry.
And the choice to heal instead of harm.

After The Honeymoon Phase

We so in awe
We want to see each other all the time
On the phone morning, noon, and night
Sweet serenades
Messages that warm the heart
Conversing for hours and hours
When we see each other, we kiss and hug
like it's the last time we'll ever embrace
Can't stop smiling
Can't stop thinking about how wonderful
this is
Can't stop feeling like this is the best thing
since the creation of existence
This is it
Until this is
"Hello, oh hey. What's up?"
"Nothing, chillin. How about you?"

Silence*
Silence*
Silence*
"Oh well, let me get back to doing what I
was doing and I'll hit you up later."
No more songful greetings
When we see each other now the hugs are
a lot looser
The smiles faded a bit
The conversations are almost nonexistent
But most of us don't realize that this is
when real life hits
And sometimes, with all the shit that's
going on in the world
We just need to be around someone and sit
in silence
It doesn't mean what we have has ended
It just means we're finally meeting each
other
Really
For the first time
Our darkness is creeping into our light

And even though you make me feel good
when I see you
I'm still navigating through life
In my head, trying to make sense of it all
This here ain't new anymore
It doesn't sparkle and shine
It's not a new toy
Or a new shirt
It's been relaxing on both of our hearts
Coffee table
And we've seen it every day
So, it's routine now
You're now a part of my life
This phase can feel lonely
Like we've both switched up
Like we both don't care anymore
Maybe our minds have deceived us into
believing we're no longer interested
Maybe met someone else
Like the grass is no longer green
It's brown
Burned in the sun we used to bathe in
Baby, all we need to do is water it

Not get so caught up in what should be
Enjoy the sweet memories
But also enjoy these moments in time
Where neither of us are able to define
Whatever this phase is

"The wound is the place where the Light enters you."
~ Rumi

Through
Remembrance
Ancient Vows
Inwardly Stir

~ Amira Jennah

Love?

Love, do you really know me?
Because I've been chasing you all my life
And every time I seem to have found you
You turn into something I no longer
recognize
So, I retreat into the pit of darkness
Only to long for the temporary warmth of
you again
So, I search
You re-emerge and do what you do best
You woo me
Make me feel like I can finally let go and
just be
Tell me sweet lies and leave me with plenty
of butterflies
Tricked me into thinking this is
Real
Really, it's just my intuition
I know the truth and I never accept it
You claim to see me

You claim to understand what I've been
through
You claim to want to make me happy
Yet I am here drowning in my own tears
Choking on my own words
Suffocating on my own suppressed
emotions
Because I love
Which cannot be returned to me
I must give and give and give
of myself
Letting pieces of me fall and fade away
into oblivion
While I support those who are that which
they are
So now… Who am I
Love, do you really know me?
How could you not after I've shown you
countless times
How can you ignore when I scream out in
pain
After the salt fills my wounds
Why, when I tell you that it hurts

You do it anyway
When I celebrate my dreams
You act as if nothing happened
When I tell the world of your presence
You act as if I don't exist
I guess that's it
I am but a stranger to you
Because love
love... love...

What is love...
really?

If there's no trust, is it love? If there's no reciprocity... no consideration, no support, no passion, no compassion, can we still call it love?

Too often, we confuse the comfort of companionship with the depth of connection.

We jump into love before understanding our own desires, then blame others when they fail to meet needs we never even shared. We say "no expectations," but the truth is, everyone is expecting something. It's human nature. We enter relationships half-authentic, pursuing people we know we aren't truly compatible with because we're chasing curiosity or validation, not commitment.

We lie to ourselves and to them, trying to control what was never meant to be controlled. Real love requires study.
It asks: Can I love this person the way they need to be loved? If the answer is no, the loving thing is to let them go. If the answer is yes, but it requires growth, then grow.
That's love. A fair exchange.

An exchange of sacrifice, honesty, and wholehearted presence. Still, sometimes we don't know what we're truly capable of until we're already in connection with someone. Self-awareness isn't just something we find alone. It can unfold inside relationships too. That's why we need both clarity and grace.

We must give ourselves and others the room to learn, to stumble, to evolve without causing harm in the process.
Let's stop performing love. Let's become it.

Finally

You dismantled the wall around my heart
Brick by brick
Then you showed me
It was never broken
Nothing needed to be fixed
I just needed to truly be loved
Not dismissed
Or shrunken
Just properly cared for
Like the prize I was
I mean the prize I am
What I needed was a human heart
And not someone trying to convince the
world
That they're a man
Someone secure
And steadfast
Someone honest
And unabashed
Someone who sees the storm in my eyes

And chooses to chase the tornado
Someone who doesn't flinch at my fire
But warms his hands in its glow
Someone who hears the trembling in my
silence
And responds with presence and not pride
I needed someone
Who doesn't mistake softness for
weakness
or independence for distance
Someone who doesn't ask me to shrink
to fit the space he's afraid to grow into
I needed a love
That didn't arrive with heavy conditions
but instead with consistency
A love that didn't feel like a performance
but like home
Now I know
I was never too much
I was never too hard to hold
I was simply waiting for the hands
that knew how to hold without hurting

I Have Seen Affection's Nectar

Tasted its sweetness on my tongue
Felt it's intensity in my heart
It's purity in my spirit

I crave for it everyday
& I will accept nothing less

@amirajennah

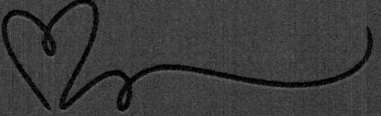

The Garden and the Flame

Once, there was a woman who wandered through a vast garden. Each flower she passed whispered of what love could be, but none ever spoke her name.

Then one day, beneath the hush of twilight, a flame flickered in the distance. It wasn't a large fire; it was gentle, contained. Warm. She stepped closer, drawn by the familiarity of its glow. As if her soul remembered something her mind had long forgotten.

The flame belonged to a man. A keeper of a different kind of fire. One who had built walls around his own heart for protection. He didn't offer the woman the whole blaze, only sparks. Oh, how those sparks sang to her spirit. With each encounter, she gave a piece of her light, hoping it would reflect enough for him to see her clearly.

She saw the goodness in him. The war within him. The love he didn't yet know how to hold. Still, she stayed. Not to fix, not to force, but to feel. For the first time, love didn't feel like survival. It felt like coming home. Yet, the man was not ready. The garden in him still had thorns, and the paths he walked were winding. So, he stepped back, choosing silence over certainty, confusion over commitment.

The woman? She did not chase. She did not rage. She became a garden of her own. A keeper of light. Still, somewhere deep inside her, a quiet whisper remains:

"This story is not over. The page is simply paused."

For some souls are chapters,
And some are whole books,
Still being written

In the ink of mystery
And the language of divine timing.

I See You

You laugh and you smile
Tell a story of hilarious sounding accidents
That just don't add up to those bruises
They laugh
While poking fun at your clumsiness but
I see you
Your eyes tell a different story
One I've experienced
So even though you're still smiling
I cry for you
Because I remember
I remember the excuses I made
For love that hurt
I remember the shame I felt
Eyes peering right through my lies
I see you
Caked-up make-up
Barely concealed bruises
I see you

You wonder why
I'm not laughing with you
Why I walked away
When you made those false statements
Why I was silent during your vent
You didn't hear my pleas
I begged you not to become me
Promise was made
With crossed fingers
You jumped back into the ring
I see you
I remember when I used to hide
I remember people questioning black eyes
I would lie
Most would always see through it
Re-enacting fake scenes
As if I could prove
It wasn't what it was
But it was
They knew it
Love was just so blind
I mean, infatuation was just so blind
I mean, fear was just so blind

I thought I could see through it
But no one
Should ever have to question
How love feels
Is it supposed to burn your heart?
Black your eye?
Bruise your skin?
Blemish your securities?
Is that why they say love hurts?
Were the smiles of other lovers as fake as
mine?
Did they want to end their own life?
Just so they could prove
That they were the ones in control?
No one should ever have to question
How love feels
I know
I see you
I made it through
You can too…

Don't forget who you are

The Mirror Woman

There once was a woman who lived in a beautiful house with rotting walls. To everyone else, it looked like a dream. The curtains always swayed gracefully, and dinner was always on time. Her smile was rehearsed, her posture flawless. Yet, inside, the house whispered warnings.

Every day, she passed by a tall mirror in the hallway. She tried not to look at it. When she did, her reflection would mouth silent words, "Leave. It's not safe here." The woman would shiver and laugh it off. A haunted mirror? Ridiculous. She couldn't tell anyone. They'd think she was mad. Maybe even lock her away.

So, she continued serving, pleasing, and surviving. Until one day, after another "argument" that left her spirit bruised and her voice small, she stopped in front of the mirror. This time, she looked and wept.

The face staring back wasn't a ghost or an omen. It was her. Her own eyes, pleading. Her own voice, buried. Her own truth, waiting. There was no magic. Just a woman trapped in fear, taught to call pain love, taught to hide the bruises on her soul.

For the first time, she listened. She packed her silence. She carried her truth. And she walked away. The house didn't collapse behind her, but something inside her finally stood tall.

Every time she sees a mirror now, she smiles at her reflection and whispers, *"Thank you for saving me."*

"Look well into thyself; there is a source of strength which will always spring up if thou wilt always look."
~ Marcus Aurelius

Black

I wear black almost every day
Some say
I wear all black to try and
compensate
For my lesser melanin
Trying to blend in
With my darker friends
As if somehow my me wearing all black
Can make me have darker skin
As if clothing could deepen my hue
Or make me more "true"
To the struggle they move through
But I know the truth
My skin grants me certain passes
Unspoken privileges in rooms
That might shut the door on others
I see it
I don't deny it
Still, I'm not pretending

My cheekbones are high,
My lips are full,
My nose…
Not Michael Jackson thin
& Not Michael Jackson wide
It's just mine
And I actually love my complexion
Not in comparison
Not in competition
Just in truth
I don't need to fit in with the crowd
Because I don't stand out
There is such a thing
As Black variety
And I am part of it
I'm not trying to "pass."
I'm trying to show up
I'm a Black woman
Not a prototype
Not a diluted version
Not a threat
Not your enemy
Don't be like Reuter,

Be like Garvey
Because how can we win the war
If we're fighting our own army?
I don't think I'm better
Than my darker sister
Because the world's gaze
Might go softer on me
And I don't think I'm lesser
For not bearing the same weight she
carries
I see the burden she walks with
The way her beauty is questioned
Her brilliance dimmed by bias
I speak her name in rooms that forget her
Because I have the privilege to
Still Black
Like my mama,
My grandmama,
And the women before her
Who had to love themselves loud
In a world that tried to silence them
I don't ignore what protects me
But I use it to protect us

So don't use my shade
To sharpen your wounds
And don't make me your excuse
For systems we both deserve to tear down
I love Black
I love being Black
Let's stop letting skin be the barrier
When love could be the bridge

Division

As humans, we often look for reasons to separate ourselves, by race, by color, by class, by creed, by gender. We divide and compete, constantly measuring our worth by how we differ rather than how we connect. In the pursuit of being "better" than others, we forget what matters most. While we fight each other, the greatest victim of our disunity is Earth itself. We ignore climate change. We ignore the growing lack of food sources. We ignore the extinction of animals, the pollution of our waters and air.

We are selfish, too busy waging social wars to come together for the one place that gives us life.

This planet is our only home. Yet we treat it as if we have somewhere else to go. We must do better. I can only pray that, one day, humanity will awaken. Not to what divides us, but to what connects us. That we'll rise together, unified, in service to each other and to this Earth we call home.

Love Thyself

To know thyself is to love thyself
But how difficult is it to learn who you are
when the world is shoving it down your
throat?
Experiences you didn't ask for shaping
who you are
How far into the darkness will your trauma
take you?
How long will the Earthquake shake you
I get it
I too have scars of
burdens that shouldn't be mine
But they are
I've searched for saviors in lovers
Needed them
To fill the voids left by others
I yearned for Disney happy endings
Unconditional love and understanding
Upset when my expectations aren't met

Unconcerned if they even had the capacity
to love me where they are
What about them?
What about me?
How frustrating it must be
Trying to squeeze apple juice from oranges
Trying to forage real love from
performances
Small annoyances
turning into huge resentment
Because we keep trying to force what is
not meant to be
The Lord is near to the brokenhearted and
saves the crushed spirit
God found me at the weakest point in my
life and told me to stop fighting
"Be still," he said
"Be Still...
So, I did
And in the stillness, I found silence
And in the stillness, I found solace
I sat with myself and myself alone

And for the first time I felt my own heart
beating
Felt my own breath entering and exiting
my body
I was aware of the space between my head
and my feet
My forehead and my chin
My shoulder and my fingertips
God showed who I am
This body
It's mine
And without it who am I?
This mind
It's mine
And I control what I allow inside
This life
It's precious…
To know thyself is to love thyself
So be careful how you treat yourself
For God is within

Come Home to Me

When I see your face
Or hear your voice
Something in me settles
Like the world hushes for a moment
I can breathe
It's your absence
That hurts the most
not loud
Lingering
I tucked a lover in my pocket
Turned away every open hand
Thinking maybe
Just maybe
You'd come back
Yet you were never mine to lose
So instead
I whisper into the quiet
Come home to me
Not to my arms
To the place I've made inside

A corner of my heart
Where you could finally rest
No judgment
No masks
Just peace
Love
The warmth I've been saving for you
You were the only man
Who never tried to sell me perfection
You showed up
As you were
Shadow and all
You let me see the parts
Most people hide
And still
I chose you
Maybe that's what scared you
Maybe that's why you left
Yet I ask myself
over and over
Why won't you let me love you?
I would give it freely
Softness, presence, devotion

All of it
And only you
Now, every time life brushes against
something that carries your scent
Your sound
Your soul
I feel it
That ache in my stomach
That longing in my chest
You live in the in-betweens
In songs
In shadows
In the pauses between breaths
Still
Despite it all
If you ever find your way back
This heart
Will be here
With the porch light on

Beautiful

I'm changing my name to beautiful
Or maybe I should change it to I Love
You
No wait, I'll change it to I Love You
Beautiful
That way every time you say my name
You'll be saying what I've been longing to
hear
I know that it
Sounds like I'm insecure
Yearning to hear words of grandeur escape
your lips leaving me with feelings that I
almost can't remember
Feelings that seemed to escape me after
years of lacking
My heart cracking a bit more at thoughts
of beautiful words escaping your lips
directed at another
And I know it
Sounds like I'm insecure

I have tears that I can't hide
Emotions I can't control
Wanting more affection yet feeling
neglected
Rejection, I don't handle well
So instead of taking this feeling of
complete and utter loneliness
Into the darkness of depression
I'll just change my name to
I Love You Beautiful
So when you call my name
I'll feel how I felt when we first met
Like I'm the apple in your eye
Instead of the thorn in your side
Giving you the stabbing pain of
complaints
Maybe it's only a temporary fix
But it'll do the trick
For the time being
At least until I need more than just the
words to get me through
And I start to yearn for your arms to hold
me too

Or maybe until you catch on to the
response I give
Do you think I'll give myself away by
saying I love you too?
It's cool
I'll be worth it
To hear you tell me on a constant basis
how you feel about me would only be a
dream come true
So from now on
Just call me
I Love You Beautiful

Now faith is the assurance of things hoped for, the conviction of things not seen.
~Hebrews 11:1

Adam & Eve

Many interpretations of the story of Adam and Eve view it as a symbolic tale of the awakening of human consciousness, especially the transition from innocence to self-awareness.

<u>The Tree of Knowledge of Good and Evil</u>
*Eating from this tree represents gaining moral awareness.
*Before eating, Adam and Eve were "naked and unashamed," symbolizing innocence.
*After eating, they realized their nakedness and felt shame, suggesting a new level of self-consciousness and awareness of dualities (good vs. evil, right vs. wrong).

<u>The Serpent</u>
Awareness:

*The serpent can symbolize curiosity, the subconscious, or the force that triggers
*It tempts Eve not just with disobedience, but with the promise of knowledge,
*"You will be like God, knowing good and evil."

The "Fall"
*The "fall" from Eden can be seen as a fall into awareness, not necessarily into sin.
*Eden may symbolize a pre-conscious state, pure existence without dualistic thinking.
*Being expelled is like being born into the human condition: aware of time, mortality, self, and others.

God's Question: "Where are you?"
*After the fall, God asks Adam, "Where are you?" A question some interpret not as about location but identity.

*It implies that with self-awareness, Adam is now disconnected from his original unity with nature and God.

Philosophical & Psychological Parallels
*In Jungian psychology, the story mirrors the development of the ego and the emergence of the conscious mind.
*In Gnostic texts, the serpent is even viewed positively, as a bringer of enlightenment.
*Existentialists might see it as the beginning of human freedom and responsibility.
So, while traditional religious interpretations focus on original sin, many spiritual, psychological, and literary readings see it as a profound metaphor for the birth of human consciousness and all the complexity that comes with it.

"Ignorance is bliss."
~Thomas Gray

I Love You

I just wanted to tell you I love you
I don't mean I love you like,
I love you for the sake of God
Or
I love you like,
I love you as just another human
I mean, I love you
From the deepest depth of my being
I love you like,
You were the letter O
With the atomic number 8
I breath you
I don't know what I did to deserve you
I was looking for love
In imperfect people
Yet, I found perfection in you
Yes
Sometimes you get on my nerves
Sometimes I trip

Over conversations not meant to win
Because you just won't let it go and
I won't let it go, but
You don't let go, and
Aggravation turns to laughter because
You hate to see me frown
So even though sorry's are scarce
The words aren't really needed
I see the apologies in your eyes
I hear
The regrets of our miscommunication
I your heartbeat
When you hold me
I know
Loving me is no easy task
I never meant to burden you with my…
Baggage
Yet, you lifted them above your shoulders
As if they were bags of feathers
Stitched me wings
From fallen pieces
Told me to soar above the bad weather
We are going to get through this

Together
Thank you
Thank you for opening every door for me
I mean that figuratively and literally
My hand never touches a handle
Because you handle everything
I just wanted to tell you that
I love you

Fixing My Own Heart: A Spiritual Framework

Healing isn't about pretending the pain never happened. It's about coming home to myself slowly, fully, and without shame. I've started to believe that wholeness is my natural state. Not perfection. Not being unbothered. Just being honest, present, and awake. That's where healing begins.

I sit in stillness and listen to my breath. That's where I meet God. That's where I remember that I am enough. I'm not too busy or needed or too impressive. I simply exist. I've learned that love can't just be received. It MUST be given. Freely and without fear. So, I give joy, prayers, softness, and kindness. Even when I don't receive it back right away, because that flow is where healing happens. Every choice is a seed. I ask myself often, am I planting peace or planting pain? Even in heartbreak, I try to choose the response that feels most like love, especially for myself. Sometimes the greatest healing comes when I stop fighting the moment. When I stop forcing myself to move on or be over it. I let the ache move through me. I cry and release. There's nothing wrong with still feeling something deeply. I've started praying for answers and for alignment. I don't need to have it all figured out. I just need to stay honest about what I desire and make room for it.

Letting go has been the hardest lesson. Still, I release the outcome. I trust that what's meant for me will not require me to beg, shrink, or suffer. I've come to understand that I'm here for a reason. My heart has been cracked open so that light could pour through. So, I could share what I've learned. So, I could serve in love, not just live through pain.

This is how I've begun to fix my own heart. I'm not trying to escape the wounds. I'm tending to them. Letting them teach me how to love better.

Where The Fire Went

She writes in the quiet
Before the chaos of the world
Pen pressed to paper
A riot
Fire burns into the margins of her own
becoming
A journal holds her turmoil
A space of growing truths
Where sorrow begins to take on the smell
of rose oil
And her sadness is proof
That's she's alive
With every breath
Is the chance to survive
Her poems used to tremble
Now they roar
Not for vengeance

But for freedom
She now pours into herself
No desire for co-dependency
She checks herself in the mirror
After a sweaty workout
She used to avoid these things
Now what joy they bring
Like the first signs of spring
She's blooming
She now laughs loud with friends
Remembering the times she had to pretend
That she didn't feel like attending
Any of their outings
Now she's at shows
Dancing through the echo of old
heartbreaks
Wearing joy like perfume
Wearing pain like pearls
Rebuilding her world
From falling embers…
Scripts stitched from goodbye letters
From love that never really entered
And never truly vanished

It lives in each frame
Each scene a resurrection
Of a heart mismanaged
The advantage of pain to a poet
Art formed from damage
Is healing
To the girl who thought she was broken
And the woman who knew better
She makes beauty
Out of everything that tried to break her
She gathers her grief
She spins it to gold
And builds altars from it
What once she thought worthless
She now calls it purpose
This is where the fire went
Into her hands
And throughout her voice
In her stories
In her demand for choice
Into the rhythm of her footsteps
On the long walk home
To herself

She is the flame now
She made herself proud

Bible Reflections

Patience

Isaac and Rebekah had to practice deep patience in their journey to parenthood. They waited 20 years before they were blessed with twins, Esau and Jacob.

Jacob (later named Israel) also had to endure a season of patience and growth. After deceiving his brother with the help of his mother to claim the inheritance, he spent many years away from home, living with the consequences of his actions and waiting for reconciliation.

Joseph, the son of Jacob, faced betrayal at the hands of his own brothers who sold him out of jealousy. Yet, through it all, he chose patience, understanding, and ultimately forgiveness. Rising through hardship to become a vessel of provision for the very family that had wronged him.

When someone shows you who they are, believe them

God revealed Himself to Pharaoh time and time again through Moses, with Aaron by his side. Miracle after miracle, warning after warning. Pharaoh hardened his heart, refusing to believe until it led to his own destruction.

The Israelites, too, witnessed God's power over and over again. From the parting of the sea to manna from heaven. Yet, with every new trial, they questioned His presence.

"It isn't me you're quarreling with, it's God!" Moses reminded them.

Sometimes the issue isn't the messenger, it's our refusal to accept the message.

Listening & Faith

Joshua, son of Nun, was a man of unwavering faith. He listened closely to God's commands and followed them without hesitation. He didn't question, he obeyed. Fully trusting in the divine plan.

Because of his faithfulness, Joshua was chosen to lead the Israelites into the Promised Land. A place his generation had longed for but never seen. And there, on the land he believed in, he lived out his old age in peace and purpose.

Obedience embedded in faith can carry us further than our doubts ever could.

Guard Your Weaknesses

Never reveal your weaknesses to just anyone, especially not to those who haven't proven they can protect them.

Samson, a man chosen by God and gifted with supernatural strength, shared the source of his power with two women he loved and trusted. Both betrayed him. Delilah, in particular, used his vulnerability to orchestrate his downfall, leading to his capture and eventual demise.

Love without discernment can become a trap. Trust without wisdom can cost you everything.

When All Seems Lost

When it feels like everything is falling apart, trust that God will send someone to help piece it back together.

Naomi lost her husband and both sons. Grief stricken and bitter, she believed her life was beyond restoration. She urged her daughters-in-law to return to their families, but Ruth refused to leave her side.

Ruth's loyalty became a lifeline. In time, she married Boaz, the family's guardian redeemer, and through that union, Naomi's legacy and estate were restored.

Sometimes, the person who stays when everyone else leaves is part of God's plan to redeem what was broken.

Disappointment

Saul was chosen by God to be the first king of Israel. Anointed in response to the people's desperate cry for leadership. He was given a divine opportunity, but time and again, he failed to follow God's commands.

His repeated disobedience wasn't just a mistake, it was a pattern. Eventually, Saul lost the very position God had entrusted to him.

You can't keep disappointing those who love you and expect their trust to remain. Love may be unconditional, but trust must be earned and protected.

Jealousy Can Be Your Downfall
Jealousy has the power to destroy not only relationships, but your own future.

Saul allowed envy to cloud his judgment when David began receiving more praise and recognition. Instead of celebrating David's victories for Israel, Saul viewed him as a threat and sought to kill him on multiple occasions.

Even when David had the chance to take Saul's life in a cave, he chose mercy over revenge. Still, Saul's fear and jealousy consumed him. In the end, he died by his own hand, afraid of being captured in battle.

Had Saul chosen unity over rivalry, he might have won the war and lived to see peace. Jealousy doesn't just hurt others, it can destroy you from the inside out.

God May Taketh Away, but He Will Give Greater in Return

Loss can feel like the end, but with God, it's often a turning point toward something greater.

David's heart was shattered by the loss of his son Absalom, whose rebellion and deception led to a tragic end. Yet even in grief, God's plan continued to unfold.

From that same lineage, God appointed Solomon, David's other son. Solomon would go on to become a king of wisdom, peace, and purpose, entrusted with building the temple of the Lord.

David's story reminds us that even in seasons of sorrow, God is still writing a greater legacy. What is lost may hurt, but what is to come will heal.

About the Author

Amira Jennah is a poet, storyteller, and filmmaker whose work centers around healing, self-discovery, and the alchemy of turning pain into purpose. A native of Philadelphia, she writes with a voice that is raw, spiritual, and emotionally resonant, unafraid to explore the beauty in both brokenness and becoming.

Her first book, Remember to Count Your Blessings, features four short fictional stories on gratitude, faith, and endurance through life's storms. It laid the foundation for her unique ability to weave narrative and emotion into transformative art.

Where the Fire Went, her second book, continues that journey, this time through a deeply personal lens. Blending poetry, parables, and reflections, it documents her path through heartbreak, healing, and renewal.

When she's not writing, Amira is creating black-and-white films, mentoring youth, or walking her spiritual path with honesty and intention. Her work is a living archive of lessons learned, love released, and the sacred art of starting over.

Contact Info

For bookings, interviews, readings, speaking engagements, workshops, or creative collaborations, please reach out via:

amirajennahbrand@gmail.com
Instagram: @amirajennah
267.282.1475

Serious inquiries only

Journal Reflections

Reflection Prompt: Take a moment to sit with what you've read.

Which poem, parable, or perspective stayed with you the most?
Was there a line that felt like it was written just for you?
What did it awaken in you? Memories, emotions, questions, or clarity?

Use the following pages to jot down your thoughts. Write freely.